INTRODUCTION

In an increasingly competitive market and with technology continuously evolving, the emergence of AI has brought about abundant opportunities for those who know how to leverage it.

Numerous studies and reports have been conducted by leading research organizations worldwide, providing insights into how the application of artificial intelligence (AI) in marketing can help businesses save costs and optimize performance. Here are some notable studies: McKinsey & Company has researched the impact of AI in business, including marketing. The study shows that automating marketing processes can reduce the time spent on repetitive tasks by up to 30%. This not only increases efficiency but also saves on personnel-related costs. According to a report from Gartner, marketing leaders are currently using AI to optimize campaigns, analyze customer data, and enhance the customer experience. Gartner estimates that companies implementing AI can save up to 20% in marketing costs in the first year of deployment.

Evidence of businesses applying AI: Coca-Cola has utilized AI to analyze data and predict consumer trends. They use AI technology to optimize product distribution processes, analyze customer shopping habits, and create personalized advertising content. Through data-driven predictions, Coca-Cola can adjust its marketing campaigns to meet the needs of specific markets. Netflix employs AI to analyze user viewing habits and suggest relevant movies or TV shows. This recommendation system not only helps retain users but also enhances engagement and increases viewing time, creating sustainable revenue for the company.

This book will equip you with 35 unique and practical marketing ideas, allowing you to easily apply AI technology to your business strategy. Each idea is presented clearly and in detail, enabling you to implement them immediately to create sustainable value for your brand. Whether you are an aspiring entrepreneur or an experienced marketer, the ideas in this book will open up new horizons for you in online business.

Get ready for the AI income revolution and explore its limitless potential! Start your journey of transformation and elevate your business today!

Contents

INTRODUCTION 1

Contents 3

Idea No1. Customer Psychological Analysis Using AI 5

1. Introduction 5

Idea No2. Deploying Intelligent Chatbots on Websites and Social Media 7

Idea No3. Personalizing Content Using AI 10

Idea No4. Trend Prediction Using Big Data Analysis 12

Idea No5. Automating Advertising Using AI 15

Idea No6. Customer Segmentation Using Machine Learning 17

Idea No7. Automated Content Creation Using AI 20

Idea No8. Emotional Tracking Using Data Analysis 23

Idea No9. Website Optimization Using AI 26

Idea No10. Competitive Analysis Using AI 28

Idea No11. Intelligent Product Recommendation Using AI .. 31

Idea No12. Brand Building Using AI 34

Idea No13. Revenue Prediction Using AI 37

Idea No14. Customer Surveys Using AI 39

Idea No15. Automated A/B Testing Using AI 42

Idea No16. Image Recognition Using AI 44

Idea No17. Keyword Analysis Using AI 46

Idea No18. Location-Based Marketing Using AI 49

Idea No19. Intelligent Customer Service Using AI 51

3

Idea No20. Automated Video Creation Using AI 53

Idea No21. Price Optimization Using AI 55

Idea No22. Feedback Analysis Using AI 58

Idea No23. AI in Advertising: Creating Dynamic Ads Automatically Based on Current Trends 60

Idea No24. Social Media Monitoring Using AI 62

Idea No25. Marketing Planning Using AI 65

Idea No26. Organizing Events Using AI 67

Idea No27. Channel Distribution Analysis Using AI 69

Idea No28. Evaluating ROI Using AI 72

Idea No29. Content Marketing Using AI 74

Idea No30. Analyzing Potential Customers Using AI 76

Idea No31. Predicting Customer Reactions Using AI 79

Idea No32. Running Real-Time Advertising Using AI 81

Idea No33. Multichannel Interaction Using AI 83

Idea No34. Fraud Detection Using AI 85

Idea No35. Performance Analysis Using AI 88

Idea No1. Customer Psychological Analysis Using AI

1. Introduction
Customer psychological analysis is considered one of the essential factors in building an effective marketing strategy. Understanding customers' psychology and behavior helps businesses optimize their products, services, and user experiences. Leveraging AI in psychological analysis confirms its ability to process and analyze large datasets quickly and accurately.

2. Steps to Perform Customer Psychological Analysis Using AI

Step 1: Data Collection

- **Data Sources**: Data can be collected from various sources, including:
    - Feedback from customer surveys.
    - Data from social media (posts, comments).
    - Purchase history.
    - Website browsing behavior (number of visits, time spent, interaction with content).

Step 2: Data Cleaning and Normalization

- Before proceeding with analysis, the data must be cleaned to eliminate unnecessary or erroneous information.
- Normalize the data to ensure consistency so that AI algorithms can easily process it.

Step 3: Sentiment Analysis

- **Utilizing Natural Language Processing (NLP) Algorithms**: Apply NLP to analyze the sentiment in textual data. For example:
    - Analyze customer surveys and feedback to identify positive, negative, or neutral emotions.
    - Evaluate sentiment from social media posts or comments.

Step 4: Behavior Analysis

- **Machine Learning**: Use machine learning models to analyze shopping behaviors and customer interactions. For example:
    - Classification algorithms to categorize customers into different psychological groups (such as loyal customers, potential customers, dissatisfied customers).
    - Predictive modeling to forecast future shopping behaviors based on past data.

Step 5: Create Analysis Reports

- Integrate the analysis results into a visual report that highlights customer psychological characteristics, presented through charts, tables, and data-backed arguments.
- These reports aid in making informed decisions, from product improvements to adjusting marketing strategies.

3. Practical Applications

- **Personalizing Customer Experience**: Based on psychological analysis, businesses can tailor advertising content and product recommendations according to customers' psychology.
- **Optimizing Customer Service**: Understanding customer psychology enables companies to develop more effective customer care programs, thereby enhancing satisfaction and loyalty.
- **Building Marketing Strategies**: A solid grasp of customer psychology allows businesses to develop personalized marketing campaigns targeting specific goals.

4. Benefits of Using AI in Customer Psychological Analysis

- **Increased Accuracy**: AI has the capability to analyze large and complex datasets more accurately than traditional methods.
- **Time Efficiency**: Automated analysis processes save time for businesses.

- **Improved Predictions**: Leveraging AI enables better forecasting of future customer psychological trends, helping businesses proactively adjust their strategies.

5. Conclusion

Customer psychological analysis using AI not only provides deep insights into their behaviors and emotions but also aids businesses in optimizing marketing strategies and enhancing customer experiences. By adopting the latest technologies, companies can maintain a competitive edge in an increasingly competitive market.

Implementing psychological analysis with AI is a stepping stone for sustainable and effective growth in all marketing activities in the future.

Idea No2. Deploying Intelligent Chatbots on Websites and Social Media

1. Introduction

Chatbots are a powerful tool in the realms of marketing and customer service, allowing businesses to communicate with customers quickly and effectively. Thanks to AI technology, chatbots can understand and process customer inquiries 24/7 without human intervention.

2. Steps to Deploy Intelligent Chatbots

Step 1: Define Objectives

- **Purpose of Use**: Identify the function of the chatbot, such as:
    - Answering frequently asked questions (FAQs).
    - Supporting sales and product consultation.
    - Providing information about services and promotions.
    - Assisting in problem resolution or customer complaints.

Step 2: Choose the Chatbot Platform

- Select the appropriate platform to deploy the chatbot. Some popular options include:
    - Free or paid chatbot tools like ManyChat, Chatfuel, or Zendesk.
    - Integrating the chatbot into the website through APIs from service providers.

Step 3: Develop Communication Scripts

- **Build Dialogue Scenarios**: Plan out dialogue scripts so that the chatbot can respond naturally and intelligently. This includes:
    - FAQs and corresponding answers.
    - Options for users to easily navigate (button options).
    - Special scenarios, such as when the chatbot does not understand a request and needs to direct the user to a human support agent.

Step 4: Train the Chatbot

- **Use NLP for Training**: Leverage Natural Language Processing (NLP) technology to help the chatbot understand the meaning and context of inquiries.
- Train the chatbot with various sample questions to improve accuracy and diversity in responses.

Step 5: Deploy and Test

- Deploy the chatbot on the website and various social media platforms (such as Facebook Messenger, Instagram).
- Conduct testing to ensure the chatbot operates effectively and can handle different scenarios.

Step 6: Monitor and Improve

- **Data Analysis**: Monitor the chatbot's performance based on metrics such as the number of conversations, problem resolution time, and customer satisfaction rates.
- Regularly update and improve the chatbot's content based on user feedback.

3. Practical Applications

- **Customer Support**: Chatbots can quickly respond to common inquiries, reducing the load on customer service teams and enhancing user experience.
- **Product Consultation**: Chatbots can analyze customer preferences and needs to provide suitable product recommendations.
- **Customer Interaction**: Chatbots can interact with customers across multiple platforms, providing businesses with opportunities to reach a broader audience of potential customers.

4. Benefits of Deploying Chatbots

- **Time and Cost Savings**: The cost of maintaining and operating a chatbot is typically lower than employing direct customer support staff.
- **Improved Customer Experience**: Customers can receive immediate responses, enhancing their satisfaction.
- **24/7 Operation**: Chatbots operate continuously, allowing businesses to support customers at all times.

5. Conclusion

Deploying intelligent chatbots on websites and social media is an effective solution that helps businesses enhance customer service quality and optimize workflows. Chatbots not only save time and costs but also provide an excellent experience for customers, thereby increasing customer loyalty and business revenue.

The development and operation of chatbots should be a crucial part of every business's marketing and customer service strategy in the digital age.

Idea No3. Personalizing Content Using AI

1. Introduction

Content personalization is an essential marketing strategy that enhances engagement and builds customer loyalty. By using AI to personalize email marketing and website content, businesses can create unique experiences for each customer, making them feel valued and more satisfied.

2. Steps to Implement Content Personalization Using AI

Step 1: Collect Customer Data

- **Data Sources**: Gather data from various sources to gain a comprehensive understanding of customers, including:
    - Personal information (age, gender, location).
    - Purchase history and website behavior (products viewed, time spent).
    - Feedback from surveys or customer interactions.

Step 2: Analyze Data

- **Use AI for Analysis**: Apply machine learning and data analysis algorithms to better understand customer preferences and behaviors. This enables businesses to categorize customers into different groups based on interests and needs.

Step 3: Create Personalized Content

- **Email Marketing**:
    - Develop email campaigns based on the preferences of each customer group. For example, send promotional information only to customers

who frequently purchase products in a specific category.
- Use customers' names in the subject line and body of the email to create a more personal connection.
- **Website Content**:
  - Personalize advertising banners and product images based on customer interests. For instance, if a customer frequently searches for running shoes, the website can showcase related sports products.
  - Utilize AI to recommend relevant content on the website, such as blog articles, videos, or products that align with the customer's search history.

Step 4: Optimize User Experience

- **Email Sending Times**: Use AI to analyze when customers are most likely to open emails and schedule the send times accordingly.
- **A/B Testing**: Conduct A/B testing to see which version of personalized content performs better. This helps optimize the effectiveness of marketing campaigns.

Step 5: Monitor and Adjust

- **Performance Analysis**: Track metrics such as open rates, click-through rates, and conversion rates to evaluate the effectiveness of personalization campaigns.
- **Update and Adjust**: Based on analysis results, update content and refine personalization strategies to align with changing customer demands and preferences.

3. Practical Applications

- **Increase Open Rates and Conversion Rates**: Personalized content significantly boosts email open rates and click-through rates.
- **Enhance Customer Loyalty**: When customers feel that content is tailored to their interests, they are more likely to return, thereby increasing brand loyalty.

- **Improve User Experience**: Personalized website content helps customers easily find information or products that they are interested in.

4. Benefits of Using AI in Content Personalization

- **Accuracy and Efficiency**: AI can provide deeper insights into customer behaviors, allowing businesses to create more accurate and compelling content.
- **Increased Flexibility**: AI enables businesses to easily adjust personalized content based on the latest customer feedback and behaviors.
- **Time Savings**: The AI-driven personalization process helps save time for marketing teams and enhances work efficiency.

5. Conclusion

Personalizing content using AI not only helps businesses create unique experiences for each customer but also optimizes the effectiveness of marketing campaigns. By employing AI technologies to understand and predict customer preferences, businesses can enhance loyalty and revenue. This approach is becoming increasingly important in the context of an increasingly competitive market.

Idea No4. Trend Prediction Using Big Data Analysis

1. Introduction

Trend prediction is a crucial part of business planning that helps companies understand shifts in consumer behavior and market dynamics. Analyzing big data enables organizations to uncover behavior patterns, demands, and emerging trends, allowing for more accurate decision-making for the future.

2. Steps to Implement Trend Prediction Using Big Data Analysis

Step 1: Data Collection

- **Data Sources**: Gather data from various sources to gain a comprehensive view of consumer trends:
    - Social media data (posts, comments).
    - Transaction data (purchase history, order records).
    - Market survey data.
    - Data from reports and industry research.

Step 2: Data Cleaning and Normalization

- Before analysis, the data needs to be cleaned to remove unnecessary or erroneous information.
- Normalize the data to ensure consistency, which is crucial for the effectiveness of analytical algorithms.

Step 3: Data Analysis Using AI

- **Utilize Machine Learning Technology**: Apply machine learning algorithms to detect patterns in big data. Techniques include:
    - Regression Analysis: used to predict variables related to sales, such as the impact of pricing on demand.
    - Clustering: to identify customer groups with similar behaviors and thus determine consumer trends within those groups.

Step 4: Build Predictive Models

- **Create Predictive Models**: Based on the analyses conducted, build predictive models to forecast future trends. These models may include:
    - Time-series forecasting: aimed at predicting sales over time.
    - Logistic regression: to predict the likelihood of customers making a purchase based on certain variables.

Step 5: Test and Refine the Models

- **Evaluate Accuracy**: Use known data to test and assess the accuracy of the model. This helps to identify errors and adjust the model for improved accuracy.
- **Refine the Model**: Based on test results, adjust the model's input factors to enhance accuracy and predictive capability.

Step 6: Apply Results to Business Strategy

- **Data-Driven Strategy Development**: Use predictions to develop marketing strategies, product offerings, and inventory management approaches.
- **Monitor and Adjust**: Continuously monitor market fluctuations and adjust the models as necessary to ensure the accuracy of predictions.

3. Practical Applications

- **Identifying Consumer Trends**: Predict new consumer trends and adjust products/services accordingly.
- **More Efficient Inventory Management**: Anticipating the necessary stock helps businesses manage inventory more effectively and reduce waste.
- **Informed Decision-Making**: Provide detailed insights for investment, marketing, and product development decisions.

4. Benefits of Using Big Data in Trend Prediction

- **Ability to Process Large Volumes of Data**: Big data allows for the analysis of large amounts of information that traditional methods cannot handle.
- **Higher Accuracy**: Predictive models based on big data analysis tend to yield more accurate results compared to traditional methods.
- **Quick Response Times**: Businesses can rapidly adapt to trends and changes in the market.

5. Conclusion

Trend prediction through big data analysis is a powerful tool that helps businesses understand shifts in consumer behavior and market dynamics. By leveraging modern technologies and analytical methods, companies can make timely and strategic decisions, maintaining a competitive edge in an increasingly competitive market. This approach not only optimizes business operations but also enhances the ability to serve customers effectively.

Idea No5. Automating Advertising Using AI

1. Introduction

Advertising automation is becoming an increasingly popular trend in digital marketing. By leveraging AI, businesses can optimize their advertising campaigns on platforms like Google Ads and Facebook Ads, helping to save time, enhance ad effectiveness, and reduce costs.

2. Steps to Implement Advertising Automation Using AI

Step 1: Set Advertising Objectives

- **Define Goals**: Before implementing automation, businesses need to identify specific advertising goals, such as:
    - Increasing website traffic.
    - Boosting conversion rates.
    - Enhancing brand awareness.

Step 2: Data Collection and Analysis

- **Gather Data**: Collect data from previous campaigns and customer interactions to inform AI algorithms. Data sources may include:
    - User behavior data.
    - Ad performance from past campaigns.
    - Demographics and interests of the target audience.

- **Analyze Data**: Utilize AI to analyze the collected data, identifying behavioral patterns and factors affecting ad performance.

Step 3: Set Up Advertising Campaigns

- **Create Ad Content**: Develop and optimize ad content for each audience segment based on the data analysis.
- **Choose Advertising Platforms**: Decide which platforms to run ads on, such as Google Ads, Facebook Ads, or Instagram, based on the target audience.

Step 4: Automate Advertising Processes

- **Use AI for Ad Optimization**: Implement AI tools to automate advertising processes, such as:
    - Optimizing cost-per-click (CPC) and cost-per-acquisition (CPA) based on real-time data.
    - Automatically adjusting budgets and allocating funds to better-performing ads.
    - Utilizing AI to generate ad suggestions based on user preferences and behaviors.

Step 5: Monitor and Evaluate Performance

- **Track Results**: Use analytical tools to monitor ad performance in real-time. Assess metrics such as click-through rates (CTR), conversion rates, and return on investment (ROI).
- **A/B Testing**: Conduct A/B testing to evaluate different ad variations and identify the most effective version.

Step 6: Adjust and Optimize

- **Analyze Outcomes**: Use the collected data to adjust advertising campaigns, improving content, targeting, and budgeting.
- **Continuous Optimization**: Leverage AI for ongoing optimization of ads based on the latest data and market feedback.

3. Practical Applications

- **Campaign Performance Optimization**: AI can predict and adjust budgets to allocate resources to the highest-performing ads.
- **Personalizing User Experience**: Delivering ads that better match individual audience segments increases engagement and conversion probabilities.
- **Managing Multiple Campaigns Simultaneously**: Businesses can run multiple advertising campaigns across different platforms without manual intervention, saving time and resources.

4. Benefits of Using AI in Advertising Automation

- **Time Savings**: Automation reduces manual work and saves time for marketing teams.
- **Enhanced Ad Effectiveness**: AI optimizes budgets and targets ads to the right audience, increasing conversion rates.
- **Cost Reduction**: By optimizing campaign performance, businesses can minimize advertising expenses while still achieving favorable results.

5. Conclusion

Automating advertising with AI is a powerful solution that helps businesses optimize their advertising campaigns on platforms like Google Ads and Facebook Ads. Utilizing big data analysis, AI not only saves time and costs but also improves advertising effectiveness. Companies can easily adjust and optimize their advertising strategies, ultimately enhancing performance and achieving desired business goals. The future of advertising automation will continue to be a significant factor in helping businesses compete in the marketplace.

Idea No6. Customer Segmentation Using Machine Learning

1. Introduction

Customer segmentation is a crucial part of modern marketing strategies that helps businesses better understand their customers. By using machine learning, companies can classify customers into specific groups based on their characteristics and behaviors. This enables optimization of marketing campaigns, enhances targeting effectiveness, and improves user experience.

2. Steps to Implement Customer Segmentation Using Machine Learning

Step 1: Collect Customer Data

- **Data Sources**: Gather data from various sources to gain a comprehensive view of customers. Data may include:
    - Personal information (age, gender, location).
    - Transaction history (previous purchases, spending amounts).
    - Website behavior (time spent, products viewed, content interactions).
    - Feedback from surveys or social media.

Step 2: Clean and Normalize Data

- **Data Processing**: This includes removing incomplete information and outlier values, and normalizing variables to ensure consistency. Clean and structured data helps improve the accuracy of the machine learning model.

Step 3: Analyze Data and Select Features

- **Data Analysis**: Utilize statistical methods and visualization to analyze the data and gain insights. Identify the most important factors (features) for customer segmentation.
- **Feature Selection**: Choose the most relevant features to use in the classification model, such as age, spending level, and interaction behavior.

Step 4: Choose a Machine Learning Model

- **Model Selection**: There are various machine learning models that can be used for customer segmentation, including:
    - **K-means clustering**: An unsupervised algorithm commonly used to group customers based on similarity.
    - **Decision Trees**: This model helps classify customers based on specific characteristics.
    - **Random Forest**: Utilizes multiple decision trees to improve accuracy and reduce overfitting.
    - **Support Vector Machines (SVM)**: A powerful classification technique that finds the best "boundaries" between groups.

Step 5: Train the Model

- **Supervised Learning**: Use labeled data to train the model, enabling it to learn how to classify based on customer attributes.
- **Testing and Refinement**: Use test data to evaluate the model's accuracy and adjust parameters to improve performance.

Step 6: Apply the Model and Segment Customers

- **Apply the Model to New Data**: Use the trained model to classify customers based on new data.
- **Create Segmentation Groups**: Divide customers into specific groups based on classification results, such as loyal customers, potential customers, or dissatisfied customers.

3. Practical Applications

- **Understanding Customers**: Through segmentation, businesses can gain deeper insights into the needs and behaviors of each customer group.

- **Optimizing Marketing**: Customer segmentation aids in customizing marketing campaigns, improving performance and increasing conversion rates.
- **Product Development**: Based on segmentation insights, businesses can develop products or services that meet the needs of specific customer groups.

4. Benefits of Applying Machine Learning in Customer Segmentation

- **Increased Accuracy**: Machine learning can process large volumes of data and identify patterns that humans might overlook.
- **Enhanced Behavioral Pattern Detection**: Helps businesses detect emerging trends and new consumer behaviors early.
- **Time and Resource Savings**: Automating the segmentation process saves time for marketing teams and data analysts.

5. Conclusion

Customer segmentation using machine learning is a powerful tool for businesses to enhance their understanding of customers and optimize marketing strategies. By applying scientific methods and modern technology, companies not only improve marketing effectiveness but also boost customer satisfaction through more tailored products and services. Customer segmentation is a critical step in building sustainable relationships with customers in an increasingly competitive environment.

Idea No7. Automated Content Creation Using AI

1. Introduction

Automated content creation is becoming an important trend in content marketing, helping businesses save time and resources. By using AI tools, companies can quickly and efficiently generate blog content or articles for marketing campaigns. This not only enhances productivity but also ensures consistency in brand messaging.

2. Steps to Implement Automated Content Creation Using AI

Step 1: Define Topics and Content Goals

- **Choose Topics**: First, businesses need to identify the topics they want to explore in their content. These topics should relate to the company's products, services, or issues that concern customers.
- **Set Goals**: Establish specific objectives for the content, such as increasing website traffic, building brand awareness, or targeting a specific audience.

Step 2: Select AI Content Creation Tools

- Numerous AI tools are available on the market capable of generating content automatically, such as:
    - **GPT-3**: A powerful language model that allows for the generation of natural text based on specific inputs.
    - Copy.ai: A dedicated tool for creating marketing content, including ad copy and blog posts.
    - **Jarvis (Jasper.ai)**: Helps generate content, write blog posts, product descriptions, and other types of material.

Step 3: Provide Input Information for the AI Tool

- **Give Specific Instructions**: Provide clear and specific input information to the AI tool, including:
    - The title and a brief description of the content.
    - Main and secondary keywords to focus on.
    - The target audience and desired writing style (formal, informal, professional, friendly, etc.).

Step 4: Generate Content

- **Use the AI Tool**: Enter the input information into the AI tool and start the content generation process. The tool will

automatically analyze and generate content according to the requirements.
- **Quality Control**: Although AI can rapidly create content, businesses should evaluate the quality to ensure it accurately reflects their brand messaging and values.

Step 5: Edit and Optimize Content

- **Review and Edit**: A writer or marketing team should review the content produced by the AI for editing and improving the tone, structure, and accuracy.
- **SEO Optimization**: Ensure that the content is optimized for search engines by integrating keywords naturally and improving the content structure with headings, H1, H2 tags, and meta descriptions.

Step 6: Publish and Promote Content

- **Publish the Content**: Once edited and optimized, the content can be published on the company's blog or website.
- **Promote the Content**: Use social media channels, email marketing, and online advertising to launch and drive the content to the target audience.

3. Practical Applications

- **Blog Writing**: Create high-quality blog content regularly, helping to enhance SEO and attract customers.
- **Survey and Analysis Articles**: Produce accessible and engaging content for in-depth industry analysis or market surveys.
- **Social Media Content**: Generate content for social media platforms to strengthen the brand's online presence.

4. Benefits of Using AI in Automated Content Creation

- **Time Savings**: Automating the content creation process significantly reduces the time needed to produce new content.
- **Increased Efficiency**: AI tools can quickly and uniformly generate large volumes of content, ensuring brand consistency.
- **High Customizability**: AI can create content that fits specific requirements and adapts to the needs of businesses and clients.

5. Conclusion

Automated content creation using AI is a powerful tool that helps businesses optimize their content production process, thereby enhancing marketing efficiency. By leveraging modern technologies, companies can not only save time and costs but also improve brand presence and enhance customer engagement. Integrating AI into content strategy will continue to be an essential factor in helping businesses compete effectively in an evolving market.

Idea No8. Emotional Tracking Using Data Analysis

1. Introduction

Tracking customer emotions is a crucial part of brand management and modern marketing strategies. By analyzing emotions from social media posts and customer feedback, businesses can better understand how customers feel about their products and services. This not only helps improve customer relationships but also assists in adjusting marketing strategies based on market feedback.

2. Steps to Implement Emotional Tracking

Step 1: Data Collection

- **Data Sources**: Gather data from various social media platforms like Facebook, Twitter, Instagram, and product review sites. The data may include:

- Customer posts (tweets, comments, articles).
- Reviews and comments on products from e-commerce sites.
- Participation and feedback from surveys and polls.

Step 2: Data Cleaning

- **Data Processing**: The collected data needs to be cleaned to eliminate unnecessary information, such as spam or irrelevant posts. The cleaning process helps increase the accuracy of the sentiment analysis.

Step 3: Sentiment Analysis

- **Utilize Sentiment Analysis Tools**: Implement tools and machine learning algorithms to analyze sentiment. Commonly used tools include:
  - **Sentiment Analysis**: Analyzing keywords and language used in posts to determine whether the sentiment is positive, negative, or neutral.
  - **Natural Language Processing (NLP)**: A branch of AI that helps computers understand human language, effectively classifying and analyzing posts.

Step 4: Evaluate and Classify Emotions

- **Determine Emotion Metrics**: Based on the analysis results, create metrics reflecting the overall sentiment of customers, such as positive, negative, and neutral sentiment scores.
- **Classify Opinions**: Group customer opinions into categories, such as satisfied customers, dissatisfied customers, and neutral customers.

Step 5: Data Visualization

- **Charts and Dashboards**: Build charts and dashboards to clearly display the results of the sentiment analysis.

Tools like Tableau and Power BI can help visualize the data effectively.
- **Periodic Reporting**: Create periodic reports to track changes in customer sentiment over time.

Step 6: Analyze and Adjust Strategies

- **Analyze Behavioral Patterns**: Based on the analyses performed, identify emotional behavior patterns of customers to adjust marketing strategies.
- **Feedback From Customers**: Use sentiment insights to develop plans for improving products, services, and customer experiences.

3. Practical Applications

- **Enhance Brand Management**: Understanding customer emotions allows businesses to manage their brand more effectively by identifying issues early and responding promptly.
- **Improve Products and Services**: Sentiment analysis helps identify aspects needing improvement in products or services based on customer feedback.
- **Engage Positively with Customers**: Leveraging obtained sentiments, businesses can tailor marketing messages and positively interact with customers.

4. Benefits of Emotional Tracking

- **Timely Capture of Customer Sentiments**: Sentiment analysis technology enables businesses to promptly monitor and assess customer perceptions.
- **Increased Customer Satisfaction**: Understanding customer emotions helps improve services and products, thereby enhancing the customer experience.
- **Data-Driven Decision Making**: Using customer sentiments to make more accurate marketing and business strategy decisions.

5. Conclusion

Tracking customer emotions through data analysis is a powerful tool for businesses to improve relationships with customers and adjust marketing strategies. By applying modern technology, businesses can accurately capture customer perceptions, leading to practical strategies that build customer loyalty and enhance brand value. Emotional tracking is not only an analytical tool but also an essential part of the overall business strategy..

Idea No9. Website Optimization Using AI

1. Introduction

Website optimization is a critical factor in enhancing user experience and improving the performance of online marketing campaigns. By using artificial intelligence (AI), businesses can effectively assess and improve user experiences on their websites. AI not only helps identify issues but also suggests optimization solutions based on actual data about user behavior.

2. Steps to Implement Website Optimization Using AI

Step 1: Collect User Data

- **Utilize Web Analytics Tools**: Implement analytics tools like Google Analytics, Hotjar, or Crazy Egg to track user behavior on the website. Collected information may include:
    - Average time spent on pages.
    - Bounce rates.
    - Most visited pages.
    - Scrolling behavior and interaction with page elements.

Step 2: Analyze Data and Identify Issues

- **Data Processing**: Use AI to analyze user behavior patterns, identifying trends and potential issues. AI tools capable of processing and analyzing large datasets can uncover problems such as:
    - Slow-loading pages.

- Lack of necessary information.
- Images or videos that do not engage or attract attention.

Step 3: Optimize Content and Design

- **Enhancing User Experience**: Based on data analysis, use AI to suggest improvements for content and website design. Some adjustments may include:
    - Improving website navigation structure to help users find information more easily.
    - Optimizing content for keywords and SEO to enhance search rankings and increase traffic.
    - Personalizing user experience based on individual behavior, such as recommending related content or products based on browsing history.

Step 4: A/B Testing Optimization

- **Conduct A/B Testing**: Use AI to perform A/B tests on website elements such as headlines, images, call-to-action (CTA) buttons, and layouts. AI helps to automate this process, allowing businesses to compare performance between different versions.
- **Analyze Results**: Monitor and analyze the results from tests to determine which version performs better. Adjust the website design accordingly based on feedback.

Step 5: Continuous Monitoring and Improvement

- **Real-Time Analytics**: Deploy AI for real-time monitoring of user behavior, allowing businesses to quickly identify and address emerging issues.
- **Regular Analysis**: Periodically review and update the optimization process based on the latest customer feedback and data. AI can help predict trends and suggest ongoing improvements.

3. Practical Applications

- **Improve Conversion Rates**: Optimize the website with the goal of increasing conversion rates, making it easier for clients to complete transactions or sign up.
- **Enhance Customer Experience**: Ensure that the website operates smoothly and is easily accessible, creating a positive experience for users.
- **Explore Customer Behavior**: Analyzing user behavior helps businesses understand the strengths and weaknesses of their websites, leading to improved services and products.

4. Benefits of Website Optimization Using AI

- **Time and Cost Efficiency**: Using AI saves time for technical and marketing teams in data collection and analysis.
- **Enhanced Website Performance**: AI helps quickly identify and resolve issues, ensuring optimal website operation.
- **Improved Customer Satisfaction**: Optimizing user experiences leads to greater customer satisfaction and loyalty.

5. Conclusion

Website optimization using AI is a powerful strategy that not only enhances user experiences but also improves overall marketing performance. By leveraging modern technology, businesses can adjust strategies based on insights from data, thereby increasing efficiency and customer satisfaction. Optimization is not just a one-time process but a continuous journey to deliver the best value to users and businesses alike.

Idea No10. Competitive Analysis Using AI

1. Introduction

Competitive analysis is a crucial element in developing effective marketing strategies. By utilizing artificial intelligence (AI), businesses can accurately and quickly monitor and analyze their competitors' marketing strategies. AI provides valuable insights into how competitors interact with customers, the methods and platforms they use, enabling businesses to adjust their strategies to optimize opportunities for success.

2. Steps to Implement Competitive Analysis Using AI

Step 1: Identify Competitors for Analysis

- **Select Competitors**: Businesses need to identify key competitors within the industry and those with similar business models. Competitors can include both major brands and smaller players with significant influence.

Step 2: Gather Market Data

- **Online Data**: Use AI to collect data from various sources, including:
    o Competitors' official websites.
    o Social media platforms (Facebook, Instagram, Twitter).
    o Consumer reviews, articles, and comments.
    o Industry reports and analyses.

Step 3: Analyze Content and Marketing Strategies

- **Content Analysis**: Use AI tools to analyze competitors' content, including:
    o Primary and secondary keywords they use for SEO.
    o Messaging strategies and branding styles.
    o Types of content produced (articles, videos, images) and publishing frequency.
- **Effectiveness Analysis**: Evaluate the effectiveness of competitors' marketing campaigns using metrics like social media engagement, conversion rates, and customer feedback.

Step 4: Monitor Advertising and Media Campaigns

- **Advertising Analysis**: Use AI to track the ads competitors place on platforms like Google Ads or Facebook Ads, analyzing their approaches and target audiences.
- **Performance Tracking**: Monitor the performance of competitors' advertising campaigns, including click-through rates (CTR), cost per click (CPC), and engagement with advertising content.

Step 5: Evaluate KPIs and Overall Performance

- **Identify KPIs**: Establish key performance indicators (KPIs) to measure competitors' success. These metrics may include:
  - Website traffic.
  - Social media interactions.
  - Revenue and customer retention rates.
- **Comparison**: Compare competitors' performance against business KPIs to identify areas for improvement.

Step 6: Analyze and Develop Strategies

- **Create Detailed Reports**: Summarize findings and analysis in a comprehensive report, highlighting competitors' strengths and weaknesses.
- **Adjust Strategies**: Based on the information gathered, adjust the marketing strategies of the business to capitalize on market opportunities and create competitive advantages.

3. Practical Applications

- **Improve Content Strategy**: Understanding competitors' content and strategies allows businesses to develop more compelling and competitive content.
- **Optimize Advertising**: Analyzing competitors' advertising campaigns helps businesses optimize advertising budgets and identify the most effective communication channels.

- **Build Brand Identity**: Gaining insights into how competitors build and maintain their brands will help businesses develop a stronger branding strategy.

4. Benefits of Competitive Analysis Using AI

- **Increased Information Gathering Speed**: AI automates the data collection and analysis process, saving time and effort for marketing teams.
- **Identify Market Trends**: AI can detect prominent trends that competitors are leveraging, allowing businesses to quickly adapt and seize opportunities.
- **Data-Driven Decision Making**: Information gathered from competitor analysis supports businesses in making strategic decisions based on real data.

5. Conclusion

Competitive analysis using AI is a powerful tool that helps businesses gain a deeper understanding of the market and their position within it. By applying modern technology in the data collection and analysis process, businesses can create effective marketing strategies, thereby increasing their competitive edge and creating sustainable growth opportunities in the marketplace. Analyzing competitors not only helps improve current strategies but also shapes the future development of the business.

Idea No11. Intelligent Product Recommendation Using AI

1. Introduction

Intelligent product recommendation is one of the most popular applications of artificial intelligence (AI) in the e-commerce and retail industry. By analyzing customers' shopping history and behavior, AI can suggest the most relevant products, enhancing user experience and increasing conversion rates. This system not only helps businesses boost revenue but also creates value for customers by providing options that match their needs and preferences.

2. Steps to Implement Intelligent Product Recommendation

Step 1: Collect Customer Data

- **Shopping History Data**: Gather data related to customers' transaction histories, including:
  - Products purchased.
  - Time and frequency of purchases.
  - Average order value.
  - Demographic information (age, gender, geographic location).

Step 2: Analyze Data and Understand Customer Behavior

- **Utilize AI Technology**: Apply machine learning algorithms to analyze the data and identify consumer behavior patterns. Common techniques include:
  - **Supervised Learning**: Use known data to train models to recognize products that customers are likely interested in.
  - **Unsupervised Learning**: Utilize clustering to find groups of customers with similar buying behaviors and identify popular products within each group.

Step 3: Build the Product Recommendation System

- **Recommendation Algorithms**: Implement recommendation algorithms such as Collaborative Filtering or Content-Based Filtering.
  - **Collaborative Filtering**: Based on the behaviors of similar users to suggest products. For example, if customers A and B have purchased many similar products, a product purchased by customer B that customer A hasn't bought can be recommended to A.
  - **Content-Based Filtering**: Based on the attributes of products that customers have previously purchased to suggest similar products.

Step 4: Fine-Tune and Improve the Recommendation Model

- **Performance Analysis**: Monitor and evaluate the performance of recommendations based on customer feedback and conversion rates. Key metrics to focus on may include:
  - Click-through rate (CTR) for suggested products.
  - Conversion rate (CVR) from recommendations.
- **Continuous Improvement**: Use new data to update and adjust the recommendation model to optimize accuracy and relevance of suggested products.

Step 5: Integrate Into Customer Experience

- **Product Suggestions Across Platforms**: Integrate the recommendation system into various customer touchpoints, including:
  - Product pages: Display related products.
  - Email marketing: Send product suggestions based on purchase history.
  - Shopping cart: Show additional or alternative products when customers are checking out.

3. Practical Applications

- **Increase Revenue**: An intelligent recommendation system helps boost revenue by encouraging customers to purchase additional products.
- **Enhance User Experience**: Customers feel more comfortable receiving relevant product suggestions, creating a positive impression of the brand.
- **Reduce Bounce Rates**: Helps keep customers on the website longer by providing related content.

4. Benefits of Using Intelligent Product Recommendations

- **Increased Personalization**: Product suggestions create a personalized experience for customers, which is extremely important in building loyalty.
- **Data-Driven Decisions**: AI helps businesses make decisions based on real consumer behavior data rather than relying solely on intuition.
- **Enhanced Competitive Edge**: Companies with intelligent recommendation systems will have a competitive advantage in an increasingly competitive e-commerce environment.

5. Conclusion

Intelligent product recommendations using AI not only benefit businesses but also enhance customer experience. By providing personalized suggestions, businesses can optimize conversion rates and build long-term relationships with customers. Implementing an intelligent product recommendation system is essential for differentiating oneself in a rapidly growing and competitive market.

Idea No12. Brand Building Using AI

1. Introduction

Brand building is an essential process for any business aiming to establish its position and increase its value in the market. In an increasingly competitive environment, discovering and capturing industry trends is crucial. By using artificial intelligence (AI) to analyze data and market trends, businesses can adjust their branding strategies flexibly and timely. This not only provides a competitive advantage but also creates a strong connection with customers.

2. Steps to Implement Brand Building Using AI

Step 1: Collect Market Data

- **Diverse Data Sources**: Gather data from various sources, including:

- Social media analysis: Monitor conversations, feedback, and comments from customers.
- Surveys and market research: Conduct surveys to collect customer opinions on the brand and products.
- Sales data: Analyze information on best-selling products compared to less effective ones.

Step 2: Analyze Data and Identify Trends

- **Utilize AI Technology**: Apply machine learning algorithms to analyze the collected data. Common techniques include:
  - **Sentiment Analysis**: Use AI to assess customer sentiments from social media posts and comments, providing insights into customer perceptions of the brand.
  - **Trend Identification**: Analyze data patterns to detect trends and shifts in consumer behavior.

Step 3: Adjust Branding Strategy

- **Developing Flexible Branding**: Use the analyzed information to adjust branding strategies in various aspects, such as:
  - Creating appropriate marketing plans: Optimize messaging and advertising campaigns based on analytical results (like customer segmentation, timing, and effective communication channels).
  - Crafting brand messaging: Tailor messaging to resonate with customer needs and expectations.

Step 4: Implement and Monitor Strategy

- **Campaign Execution**: Launch communication, advertising, and product development campaigns based on the adjusted strategy.
- **Performance Tracking**: Use AI to monitor the effectiveness of branding campaigns. Key metrics to focus on include:
  - Customer engagement and feedback.

- Conversion rates and sales figures.
- Brand awareness and market positioning.

Step 5: Continuous Improvement

- **Analyze Feedback**: Monitor customer feedback after launching branding campaigns to draw insights for future improvements.
- **Optimize the Model**: Use collected data to continually refine the branding strategy model.

3. Practical Applications

- **Enhancing Product Quality**: Capturing and responding to market trends helps businesses improve the quality and features of their products.
- **Establishing Brand Position**: Building a brand image that aligns with market trends and customer demands helps create a solid brand position in customers' minds.
- **Connecting with Customers**: Understanding customer needs and psychology fosters a close connection, thereby enhancing their loyalty to the brand.

4. Benefits of Using AI in Brand Building

- **Enhanced Predictive Capabilities**: AI helps forecast future trends based on historical data, allowing businesses to plan and adjust strategies more effectively.
- **Data-Driven Decision Making**: Businesses can make well-informed and precise decisions based on real data analysis.
- **Capacity for Large Data Processing**: AI can process vast amounts of data quickly and efficiently, enabling swift trend detection.

5. Conclusion

Building a brand using AI not only helps businesses discover industry trends but also enables timely and flexible adjustments to branding strategies. The combination of modern data analysis and intelligent business strategies will create immense value for both the brand and its customers. Implementing AI in brand building represents a significant step toward optimizing business operations and maintaining competitiveness in the marketplace.

Idea No13. Revenue Prediction Using AI

1. Introduction

Revenue prediction is a crucial part of a business's financial planning. Accurate revenue forecasting helps businesses optimize financial management, develop more effective business strategies, and allocate resources efficiently. Using artificial intelligence (AI) to analyze data and provide revenue forecasts not only improves accuracy but also speeds up the process compared to traditional methods.

2. Steps to Implement Revenue Prediction Using AI

Step 1: Data Collection

- **Diverse Data Sources**: Gather both historical and current data, including:
    - Monthly or quarterly revenue figures from previous years.
    - Sales data by product, region, and time period.
    - Information about promotions, discount programs, and advertising factors.
    - Macroeconomic indicators that may affect revenue, such as unemployment rates, consumer price indices, and GDP growth.

Step 2: Data Preprocessing

- **Data Cleaning**: Remove any inaccurate or missing data to ensure data quality at the input stage.
- **Data Transformation**: Convert data into a consistent format and type to ensure uniformity.
- **Feature Engineering**: Create relevant features from the initial data, which may include:

- Changes in revenue over time.
- Relationships between revenue and other influencing factors like market conditions or seasonal effects.

Step 3: Data Analysis Using AI

- **Select Appropriate Algorithms**: Use machine learning algorithms such as linear regression, logistic regression, decision trees, or neural networks to model the data.
- **Train the Model**: Utilize historical data to train the AI model, aiming to find the relationships between various features and revenue.

Step 4: Revenue Prediction

- **Model Testing**: Use a test dataset to evaluate the model's accuracy. Important metrics to analyze may include:
  - Mean Absolute Error (MAE).
  - Mean Squared Error (MSE).
- **Prediction**: Use the trained model to forecast future revenue based on existing input data.

Step 5: Monitor and Refine the Model

- **Performance Monitoring**: Keep track of the accuracy of revenue predictions over time to promptly identify discrepancies or shortcomings.
- **Model Improvement**: Use new data and feedback to adjust and enhance the model, making it more accurate in future predictions.

3. Practical Applications

- **Strategic Planning**: Based on revenue predictions, businesses can plan both long-term and short-term strategies, from staffing decisions to investments in new projects.

- **Inventory Management**: Revenue forecasting helps businesses manage inventory more effectively, minimizing stockouts or excess inventory.
- **Budget Optimization**: Assists businesses in allocating budgets more efficiently for marketing activities and product development based on projected revenue.

4. Benefits of Revenue Prediction Using AI

- **High Accuracy**: AI has the capability to analyze vast amounts of data and identify patterns, enhancing the accuracy of predictions.
- **Detection of Potential Trends**: AI aids in recognizing consumer trends and influencing factors on revenue that may be challenging to detect through traditional methods.
- **Data-Driven Decision Making**: Forecasts based on real data enable businesses to make informed and grounded decisions.

5. Conclusion

Revenue prediction using AI is a powerful tool that helps businesses achieve more accurate and effective financial planning. By applying machine learning algorithms and data analysis, businesses can gain crucial insights into future revenue, optimizing operations and enhancing competitiveness in the market. Implementing revenue prediction with AI not only increases the potential for business growth but also enables rapid responsiveness to market fluctuations.

Idea No14. Customer Surveys Using AI

1. Introduction

Customer surveys are an important tool for gathering opinions and feedback from consumers about products or services. Effectively analyzing survey results helps businesses better understand customer needs, desires, and expectations. Using artificial intelligence (AI) to analyze data from customer surveys not only enhances the accuracy of data processing but also helps uncover patterns of behavior and essential information for improving products or services.

2. Steps to Implement Customer Surveys Using AI

Step 1: Survey Design

- **Create Effective Questionnaires:** Design questionnaires to be clear and easy to understand, including both quantitative questions (rating systems) and qualitative questions (open-ended) to collect multidimensional data.
- **Target Audience:** Clearly identify the customer segment you want to survey, such as those who have used the product within a certain timeframe.

Step 2: Data Collection

- **Conduct the Survey:** Use online survey platforms or emails to send questionnaires to customers.
- **Encourage Participation:** Provide incentives or rewards to encourage customers to participate in the survey, such as discounts or gifts.

Step 3: Data Analysis Using AI

- **Data Preprocessing:** Process the data by cleaning and standardizing responses to ensure accuracy and consistency.
- **Utilize AI Technology:**
    - **Sentiment Analysis:** Analyze open-ended responses to gauge customer emotions and opinions, helping to identify common issues or standout strengths.
    - **Clustering:** Use algorithms like K-means to group customers based on similar characteristics, helping businesses better understand different customer segments.

Step 4: Draw Conclusions and Make Recommendations

- **Summarize Information:** Compile survey results based on the analyzed data. Key metrics to consider may include:
    - Customer satisfaction levels.
    - Common issues faced by customers.
    - Products/services highly rated by customers.
- **Provide Recommendations:** Based on findings, suggest solutions to improve products or services in alignment with customer needs and preferences.

Step 5: Implement Improvements

- **Adjust Products/Services:** Apply recommendations to enhance the products or services offered by the business.
- **Monitor Feedback:** After implementing changes, continue to monitor customer feedback to assess how these improvements have impacted customer satisfaction and revenue.

3. Practical Applications

- **Improve Product Quality:** With insights from surveys, businesses can adjust and enhance product features to meet actual customer demands.
- **Build Marketing Strategies:** Survey data can help businesses better understand customer outreach, leading to more effective marketing campaigns.

4. Benefits of Using AI in Customer Surveys

- **Enhanced Analytical Capability:** AI can quickly and accurately process and analyze large volumes of data.
- **Uncover Hidden Insights:** AI helps identify patterns and information that may not be easily recognized through manual analysis.
- **Optimize Processes:** Minimizes the time and effort needed for data analysis and report creation.

5. Conclusion

Customer surveys using AI represent an effective method for collecting and analyzing customer feedback. This allows businesses to gain deeper insights into customer needs and desires, leading to improvements in product and service quality. Implementing AI in survey analysis not only enhances accuracy but also enables businesses to swiftly adapt to market changes, increasing customer satisfaction and retention.

Idea No15. Automated A/B Testing Using AI

1. Introduction

A/B testing is an important method in digital marketing that allows businesses to compare two versions of an advertisement or landing page to determine which version performs better. Using artificial intelligence (AI) to automate the process of running and analyzing A/B tests not only saves time but also enhances accuracy in making data-driven decisions.

2. Steps to Implement Automated A/B Testing Using AI

Step 1: Define the Testing Goals

- **Select KPIs:** Clearly define the key performance indicators (KPIs) that you want to improve, such as click-through rate (CTR), conversion rate (CR), or time on page.
- **Identify the Target Audience:** Choose the user group on which you want to conduct the test and determine the sample size needed.

Step 2: Create and Run Test Versions

- **Design Variants:** Create two versions (A and B) of the advertisement or landing page, with each version having a different element you want to test (e.g., headline, image, content).
- **Automate the Process:** Use AI tools to automatically distribute traffic between the different versions evenly to ensure accuracy in the results.

Step 3: Data Collection

- **Monitor User Feedback:** Use AI to collect and analyze real-time data from visitors across both versions.
- **Record Interactions:** Track user interactions such as click counts, time spent on page, and actions taken.

Step 4: Analyze Data Using AI

- **Performance Analysis:** Use machine learning algorithms to analyze data and compare the performance of versions A and B:
  - **Statistical Testing:** Employ t-tests or other statistical methods to determine whether performance differences are significant or merely random.
  - **Detect Hidden Patterns:** AI can help identify patterns or trends in the data that may not be visible to the naked eye.

Step 5: Make Decisions and Optimize

- **Identify the Winning Version:** Based on the analysis, determine which version performed better and whether it should be implemented long-term.
- **Improve Future Campaigns:** Use the insights gained from the A/B test to optimize future advertising campaigns and landing pages.

3. Practical Applications

- **Optimize Advertising Campaigns:** Use AI to automate A/B tests on online advertising platforms like Google Ads and Facebook Ads, enhancing the effectiveness of the ads.
- **Enhance User Experience:** Improve landing pages based on user feedback, thereby elevating the overall customer experience.

4. Benefits of Using AI in A/B Testing

- **Time Savings:** Automating the process saves time and resources for the marketing team.
- **Increased Accuracy:** AI enhances accuracy in data analysis and helps detect patterns that are hard to recognize.
- **Seamless Process:** The automation of the A/B testing process creates a smooth workflow from design to analysis.

5. Conclusion

Automating A/B testing using AI is an effective approach to optimize advertising campaigns and landing pages. By automating the process from design to analysis, businesses can make quick and accurate decisions based on real data. Applying AI not only improves performance but also generates deeper insights into customer behavior, allowing businesses to enhance user experiences and increase revenue.

Idea No16. Image Recognition Using AI

1. Introduction

Image recognition is a field of artificial intelligence (AI) that allows computers to analyze and understand the content of images. Utilizing AI to analyze images and collect information from social media posts offers numerous benefits for businesses, such as capturing customer sentiment, monitoring brand presence, and detecting market trends.

2. Steps to Implement Image Recognition Using AI

Step 1: Data Collection

- **Choose Platforms:** Identify the social media platforms from which you want to collect data, such as Instagram, Facebook, Twitter, or TikTok.
- **Use Data Collection Tools:** Employ social media APIs to gather images from posts, profile pictures, or images related to the brand you wish to analyze.

Step 2: Data Preprocessing

- **Clean and Standardize Data:** Process the collected images to ensure consistency (e.g., size and format).
- **Label Data:** Define labels for the images if necessary, which aids in training the AI model.

Step 3: Image Analysis

- **Utilize Image Recognition Models:** Apply deep learning algorithms, such as Convolutional Neural Networks (CNNs), to analyze images. Common applications include:
    - **Object Recognition:** Identifying specific objects in images, such as products, logos, or people.
    - **Image Classification:** Classifying images into categories based on content or themes.
    - **Sentiment Analysis:** Detecting emotions of individuals in images, such as happiness, sadness, or anger.

Step 4: Information Gathering and Data Analysis

- **Trend Analysis:** Use the obtained data to identify trends in customer behavior, including popular products and trending topics within the community.
- **Brand Assessment:** Monitor images related to the brand and evaluate how users interact with the brand through visuals.

Step 5: Decision Making and Recommendations

- **Strategic Decisions:** Based on the analysis, identify opportunities or challenges and adjust marketing strategies accordingly.
- **Content Optimization:** Use the insights gained to adjust advertising and social media content to enhance engagement and brand recognition.

3. Practical Applications

- **Brand Management:** Use AI to monitor and analyze images related to the brand to understand how current and potential customers perceive it.
- **Market Research:** Detect new trends and customer opinions through image analysis, leading to improvements in products and services.

4. Benefits of Using AI in Image Recognition

- **Large-Scale Analysis:** AI can analyze millions of images quickly and efficiently.
- **Detailed and Accurate Insights:** Provides deep insights into how customers interact with brands and products through images.
- **Enhanced Decision-Making Capability:** Information from image analysis supports businesses in making accurate and timely decisions based on customer behavior.

5. Conclusion

Image recognition using AI is a powerful tool for collecting and analyzing information from social media posts. By analyzing images, businesses can gain deeper insights into customer attitudes and preferences, allowing them to adjust marketing strategies and develop products that better meet customer needs. Applying AI in this domain not only enhances competitiveness but also creates added value for the brand.

Idea No17. Keyword Analysis Using AI

1. Introduction

Keyword analysis is a crucial process in search engine optimization (SEO) that helps improve a website's ranking in search results. Utilizing artificial intelligence (AI) to analyze and optimize keywords not only helps identify more effective keywords but also uncovers search trends, thereby enhancing visibility and attracting traffic to the website.

2. Steps to Implement Keyword Analysis Using AI

Step 1: Data Collection

- **Utilize Keyword Analysis Tools:** Use SEO tools like Google Keyword Planner, Ahrefs, SEMrush, or Moz to gather initial data on keywords related to your industry or products.
- **Review Search Trends:** Analyze trend data from Google Trends to identify new keywords that are gaining popularity and may not have been leveraged yet.

Step 2: Keyword Analysis and Evaluation

- **Apply AI for Data Analysis:** Implement machine learning algorithms to analyze keyword data. Key factors to consider include:
  - **Monthly Search Volume:** Determine how often a keyword is searched on search engines.
  - **Competition Level:** Assess how competitive the keyword is, helping to identify the difficulty of ranking for it.
  - **Context and Search Intent:** AI can help analyze the intent behind keywords, determining what users are genuinely looking for.

Step 3: Create Optimized Content

- **Develop Content Around Keywords:** Use insights from the analysis to create high-quality content that provides value to users and is optimized for the selected keywords.
- **On-Page SEO Optimization:** Ensure that keywords are effectively used in elements such as titles, H1 tags, meta descriptions, and the main content of the page.

Step 4: Monitor and Evaluate Performance

- **Utilize Analytics Tools:** Track keyword rankings and website traffic using tools like Google Analytics and Google Search Console.

- **Adjust Keyword Strategy:** Based on the data collected, regularly adjust and optimize your keyword list to improve SEO performance.

Step 5: Detect New Trends

- **Regular Updates:** Use AI to analyze and detect new trends in keyword searches. The system can automatically suggest emerging keywords based on user search behavior.
- **Continuous Optimization:** Continuously optimize and update content and keywords to meet changes in consumer behavior and search trends.

3. Practical Applications

- **Enhance Search Rankings:** Optimizing content and keywords helps improve a website's visibility on search engines.
- **Increase Organic Traffic:** Effectively using keywords attracts organic traffic, thereby increasing conversion opportunities and revenue.

4. Benefits of Using AI in Keyword Analysis

- **Rapid and Efficient Analysis:** AI can process and analyze large volumes of data more quickly than traditional methods.
- **Deeper Understanding of Users:** AI can help businesses better understand user search intent and behavior.
- **Improved Accuracy:** Increases accuracy in identifying more effective keywords and minimizes the risk of selecting inappropriate keywords.

5. Conclusion

Keyword analysis using AI is a vital part of modern SEO strategy. By leveraging AI technology to analyze and optimize keywords, businesses can enhance their position on search engines and attract higher-quality traffic. This not only improves SEO performance but also optimizes the user experience, leading to greater conversion rates and revenue.

Idea No18. Location-Based Marketing Using AI

1. Introduction

Location-based marketing is a strategy that allows businesses to use customers' geographical information to send relevant messages, offers, or promotions. Utilizing artificial intelligence (AI) to analyze location data not only optimizes marketing campaigns but also enhances customer experiences through personalization.

2. Steps to Implement Location-Based Marketing Using AI

Step 1: Data Collection

- **Utilize GPS and Geolocation Data:** Leverage GPS technology on mobile phones and smart devices to collect location data from customers.
- **Analyze Social Media Information:** Tap into data from social media posts where users check in or share their current or past locations.

Step 2: Build Customer Segmentation Rules

- **Segment by Location:** Use AI to classify customers based on diverse geographical areas, from regions and districts to cities and nearby store locations.
- **Identify Behavioral Characteristics:** Analyze customer behavior based on location to determine the optimal times and places to send messages.

Step 3: Create Personalized Content

- **Develop Marketing Messages:** Customize messages according to the customer's location. For instance, send

special promotions to those near a store or announcements about local events.
- **Integrate with Marketing Platforms:** Use marketing automation platforms to schedule and automatically send messages or notifications based on the customer's location.

Step 4: Send Messages and Promotions

- **Utilize Push Notifications:** Send push notifications to customers when they are within the target area, such as discount alerts or promotional offers.
- **Send Emails or SMS Messages:** Send emails or text messages with invitations or offers that customers can use when visiting the store.

Step 5: Monitor and Evaluate Effectiveness

- **Analyze Customer Feedback:** Use AI to analyze the level of interaction and feedback from messages sent to customers.
- **Adjust Strategies:** Based on the analysis, adjust and optimize location-based marketing strategies for better effectiveness in future campaigns.

3. Practical Applications

- **In-Store Promotions:** Proactively send promotional messages to customers located near a store or business site.
- **Local Events:** Organize events and send invitations to customers in the area to enhance participation and engagement.

4. Benefits of Using AI in Location-Based Marketing

- **Enhanced Personalization:** Deliver messages tailored to individual customers, improving the experience and conversion rates.

- **Optimized Marketing Efficiency:** AI analyzes and predicts customer behaviors, facilitating more effective promotions.
- **Real-Time Capabilities:** The ability to send messages instantaneously based on the customer's location in real-time.

5. Conclusion

Location-based marketing powered by AI presents businesses with the opportunity to engage customers in a more personalized and effective manner. By analyzing location data, businesses can optimize their marketing campaigns, thereby enhancing customer experiences and increasing revenue. Implementing AI in this area not only improves business performance but also builds stronger relationships with customers.

Idea No19. Intelligent Customer Service Using AI

1. Introduction

Intelligent customer service leverages artificial intelligence (AI) to enhance service quality and optimize the process of handling customer inquiries. With the ability to process information quickly and accurately, AI can help businesses resolve complex issues, providing a better customer experience and increasing operational efficiency.

2. Steps to Implement Intelligent Customer Service Using AI

Step 1: Identify Customer Service Needs

- **Analyze customer inquiries:** Research common issues customers encounter through various support channels such as email, phone, and social media.
- **Identify areas for improvement:** Assess the current performance of customer service to determine inefficient processes or recurring issues.

Step 2: Deploy Chatbots and Virtual Assistants

- **Develop intelligent chatbots:** Use AI to create chatbots capable of automatically interacting with customers, answering frequently asked questions, and handling simple requests.
- **Virtual assistants for complex inquiries:** Implement virtual assistants that can address more complex requests and engage in deeper conversations with customers.

Step 3: Integrate AI Systems with Customer Data

- **Analyze customer data:** Use machine learning algorithms to analyze data from previous customer interactions to gain better insights into their behavior and needs.
- **Create customer profiles:** Develop personalized profiles for each customer based on collected information, enabling better service delivery.

Step 4: Automate Customer Service Processes

- **Manage and categorize requests:** Use AI to automatically categorize requests and route them to the appropriate departments, saving time and optimizing resources.
- **Record and track:** AI can log complaint histories and resolved issues, aiding staff in easily tracking and managing subsequent requests.

Step 5: Evaluate and Continuously Improve

- **Monitor service performance:** Use KPIs to track and analyze the performance of customer service, making necessary adjustments.
- **Gather customer feedback:** Collect feedback from customers to improve services and refine the strategy for using AI in customer service management.

3. Practical Applications

- **24/7 customer support:** Chatbots and virtual assistants can operate continuously, providing customer support anytime, anywhere.
- **Efficient complaint resolution:** AI can help identify the root cause of complaints and provide solutions quickly and accurately.

4. Benefits of Using AI in Customer Service

- **Time savings:** Automating processes reduces wait times for customers and enhances request processing speed.
- **Increased customer satisfaction:** Fast and efficient service improves the overall customer experience.
- **Handling complex inquiries:** AI can address complex situations with greater accuracy than traditional methods.

5. Conclusion

Intelligent customer service using AI not only optimizes the customer experience but also enhances operational efficiency for businesses. By applying AI to handle complex inquiries, companies can create a flexible, rapid, and effective service. This combination not only alleviates the workload on staff but also strengthens long-term relationships with customers, increasing loyalty and revenue for the business.

Idea No20. Automated Video Creation Using AI

1. Introduction

Automated video creation through artificial intelligence (AI) is becoming one of the powerful marketing trends. This technology allows businesses to transform existing content into advertising or marketing videos without requiring extensive time or resources. AI optimizes the video production process, from editing and image generation to background music selection, helping businesses save costs and enhance effectiveness.

2. Steps to Implement Automated Video Creation Using AI

Step 1: Content Gathering

- **Collect existing content:** Gather documents, articles, images, short video clips, or any resources that a business has.
- **Define video objectives:** Set clear goals for the video—whether it is a product advertisement, a usage guide, or an informative brand video.

Step 2: Select AI Technology

- **Choose automated video creation tools:** Utilize software or platforms like Lumen5, Pictory, or InVideo, which allow automation of the video production process from text and existing resources.
- **Explore advanced features:** Leverage enhanced features such as music selection, text and image addition, as well as transition effects.

Step 3: Create the Video

- **Transform content into video:** Input the content into the AI system, allowing the tool to automatically generate the video based on the chosen message and format.
- **Customize the production process:** Adjust factors like video length, editing processes, and the arrangement of clips to match the brand style.

Step 4: Review and Edit

- **Preview the video:** Check and preview the video before publishing to ensure it conveys the intended message and meets desired quality.
- **Make necessary edits:** Use editing tools to modify any parts that need improvement, such as changing images or audio.

Step 5: Publish and Promote the Video

- **Publish the completed video on various platforms:** Post the finished video on websites, social media, YouTube, or other marketing channels.
- **Promote the video:** Communicate and promote the video across different channels to enhance reach and engagement from consumers.

3. Practical Applications

- **Advertising videos:** Create short, engaging advertising videos based on the products or services the business offers.
- **Usage guides and information:** Produce instructional videos on how to use products or provide information about services in a visual and understandable way.

4. Benefits of Using AI in Automated Video Creation

- **Time and cost savings:** Minimizes the resources needed for video production, from labor costs to production time.
- **Enhanced marketing effectiveness:** Video is a powerful content format that drives engagement and inspiration, helping to enhance the effectiveness of marketing campaigns.
- **Rapid video production:** AI has the capability to produce videos quickly, allowing businesses to promptly deliver marketing messages during campaigns.

5. Conclusion

Automated video creation using AI is an effective way to enhance a business's marketing strategy. This technology not only saves time and costs but also delivers high-quality, engaging videos rapidly and easily. Businesses can harness the power of video to improve product and brand promotion, thereby increasing conversion rates.

Idea No21. Price Optimization Using AI

1. Introduction

Price optimization is a crucial strategy in marketing and revenue management, allowing businesses to adjust the prices of their products and services based on various factors such as market demand, competitor pricing, and customer behavior. Using artificial intelligence (AI) to analyze data provides businesses with the ability to adjust prices in real time, helping to maximize profits and enhance competitiveness.

2. Steps to Implement Price Optimization Using AI

Step 1: Data Collection

- **Identify data sources:** Gather data from various sources, including competitor pricing, sales data, market information, and customer sentiment from social media.
- **Data storage:** Use efficient data storage systems to manage and organize the collected data.

Step 2: Data Analysis

- **Apply AI for data analysis:** Use machine learning algorithms to analyze the collected data, identifying trends and relationships between pricing and sales performance.
- **Segment the market:** Divide the market into different segments based on customer behavior, seasonality, and competitor characteristics.

Step 3: Demand and Trend Prediction

- **Predictive modeling:** Develop predictive models using historical data and input variables to forecast future demand.
- **A/B Testing method:** Conduct A/B testing to evaluate market responses to different price levels, thereby optimizing pricing at each stage.

Step 4: Automatic Price Adjustment

- **Establish price adjustment rules:** Use AI to automatically adjust prices in real time based on factors such as fluctuations in demand, inventory levels, and competitor actions.
- **Implement dynamic pricing:** Apply dynamic pricing strategies to adjust prices based on time, location, and customer demand.

Step 5: Evaluation and Improvement

- **Monitor price performance:** Use KPIs to track the performance of adjusted prices, such as conversion rates and profit margins.
- **Adjust pricing strategies:** Based on collected data, refine and optimize pricing strategies to better meet customer needs and market changes.

3. Practical Applications

- **E-commerce sector:** Online retail websites use AI technology to adjust product prices based on competitive levels and consumer behavior.
- **Hospitality and tourism sector:** Hotel booking systems utilize AI to change room prices according to seasonality, events, and customer demand.

4. Benefits of Using AI in Price Optimization

- **Maximize profits:** Real-time price adjustments help maximize revenue from each transaction.
- **Increase flexibility:** Businesses can quickly respond to market changes and customer behavior.
- **Enhance customer experience:** Providing more reasonable prices aligned with customer expectations increases satisfaction and loyalty.

5. Conclusion

Price optimization using AI is a powerful tool for businesses looking to improve revenue management efficiency and adapt to market changes. By analyzing and adjusting prices in real time, companies can not only increase profitability but also optimize customer experiences, creating a stronger competitive edge in their respective fields.

Idea No22. Feedback Analysis Using AI

1. Introduction

Analyzing customer feedback is a crucial factor in improving a company's products and services. By utilizing artificial intelligence (AI), businesses can quickly and effectively analyze feedback from customers to better understand their needs, trends, and areas requiring improvement. This helps optimize the customer experience and enhance business efficiency.

2. Steps to Implement Feedback Analysis Using AI

Step 1: Data Collection of Feedback

- **Identify feedback sources:** Feedback data can be gathered from various sources, including customer surveys, social media, reviews on websites, emails, and online feedback forms.
- **Organize the data:** Arrange and classify information from the above sources into a single management system for easier analysis.

Step 2: Semantic Data Analysis

- **Natural Language Processing (NLP):** Use NLP algorithms to analyze and understand the content of the feedback, especially customer sentiments and opinions.
- **Classify feedback:** Employ AI to categorize feedback into themes or types (positive, negative, suggestions for improvement, and complaints).

Step 3: Extract Strategic Insights

- **Sentiment analysis:** Evaluate the overall sentiment in the feedback to determine customer satisfaction levels and areas needing improvement.
- **Identify trends:** Detect trends and behavioral patterns from the feedback data to make predictions and adjust strategies.

Step 4: Suggest Improvements

- **Generate reports:** Create detailed reports on the analysis results, highlighting strengths and weaknesses of the product/service.
- **Provide recommendations:** Based on the analysis information, propose specific improvements for products, services, or customer service processes.

Step 5: Monitor and Evaluate the System

- **Track improvements:** Measure the impact of implemented improvements by collecting new feedback from customers.
- **Enhance the analysis process:** Continuously adjust and update the analysis procedure to ensure optimization of results and customer feedback in the future.

3. Practical Applications

- **Social media feedback analysis:** Utilize AI to monitor and analyze comments, reviews, and customer feedback on social media platforms.
- **Customer surveys:** Create automated surveys and use AI to analyze results, providing valuable insights for strategic decisions.

4. Benefits of Using AI in Feedback Analysis

- **Time savings:** AI allows for quick and accurate analysis, enabling businesses to respond in a timely manner.

- **Improved accuracy:** Sentiment and semantic analysis is more precise than manual methods, helping to better understand customer perceptions.
- **Better strategic decisions:** Provides data-driven insights, allowing businesses to make informed decisions regarding product and service improvements.

5. Conclusion

Feedback analysis using AI is an effective way for businesses to better understand their customers and adjust their strategies accordingly. By deeply analyzing customer feedback, companies can improve their products and services, thus enhancing customer satisfaction and loyalty. The combination of AI and feedback analysis will help businesses maintain a competitive edge in an increasingly challenging market.

Idea No23. AI in Advertising: Creating Dynamic Ads Automatically Based on Current Trends

1. Introduction

Dynamic advertising is an increasingly popular marketing method that allows businesses to create personalized ads that automatically adjust based on user behavior and real-time trends. Utilizing artificial intelligence (AI) in dynamic advertising enables businesses to save time and resources while enhancing the effectiveness of their promotional campaigns for products or services.

2. Steps to Implement AI in Dynamic Advertising

Step 1: Data Collection

- **Identify data sources:** Data to be collected may include user behavior, personal preferences, search trends, and information from social media.
- **Manage data:** Store and organize this data in efficient data management systems, ready for analysis.

Step 2: Data Analysis

- **Use AI to analyze behavior:** Apply machine learning algorithms to identify behavioral patterns and preferences from the collected data.
- **Classify data:** Use AI to categorize user data into groups based on preferences, demographics, and consumer behavior.

Step 3: Create Advertising Content

- **Automate content creation:** Use AI tools to automatically generate advertising content tailored to each customer segment. This may include text, images, videos, and other visual elements.
- **Customize content based on trends:** AI can track current trends on social media platforms and the internet, creating relevant and engaging advertising content based on those trends.

Step 4: Distribute and Optimize Ads

- **Ad distribution:** Utilize automated advertising systems to deliver ads to the right customer segments at optimal times.
- **Optimize based on performance:** Use AI to monitor and analyze the performance of ads (such as click-through rates and conversion rates) and automatically adjust content or advertising campaigns based on the collected data.

Step 5: Evaluate and Adjust

- **Measure campaign success:** Track KPIs (Key Performance Indicators) to assess the effectiveness of the dynamic advertising.
- **Continuous improvement:** Based on feedback and real data, adjust advertising content and marketing strategies to optimize future effectiveness.

3. Practical Applications

- **Social media advertising:** Platforms like Facebook and Instagram use AI to create dynamic ads tailored to user preferences and behaviors.
- **Online advertising:** Advertisers can leverage AI to automatically generate advertising content for PPC (Pay-Per-Click) campaigns or display ads.

4. Benefits of Using AI in Dynamic Advertising

- **Enhanced personalization:** Ads become more relevant to individual customers, increasing engagement and conversion rates.
- **Time and cost savings:** Automating the process of content creation and distribution helps reduce labor costs and working hours.
- **Rapid response to changes:** AI can quickly monitor and respond to new trends and behaviors of consumers, helping businesses maintain competitiveness in the market.

5. Conclusion

Utilizing AI in dynamic advertising offers numerous benefits for businesses. It enhances customer engagement, optimizes the process of creating and distributing advertising content, thus increasing marketing campaign effectiveness. With the continued advancement of AI technology, its application in dynamic advertising will further evolve and become an integral part of businesses' marketing strategies.

Idea No24. Social Media Monitoring Using AI

1. Introduction

Social media monitoring is a crucial aspect of brand management and modern marketing strategies. With the ever-increasing amount of information on social media platforms, utilizing artificial intelligence (AI) to track and analyze activities helps businesses quickly respond to trends, customer needs, and opinions. This not only protects the brand but also optimizes the customer experience.

2. Steps to Implement Social Media Monitoring Using AI

Step 1: Define Monitoring Objectives

- **Identify key factors to monitor:** Choose important metrics such as engagement levels, customer feedback, brand perception, and keywords related to products or services.
- **Set specific goals:** Determine what the business aims to achieve through monitoring, such as improving customer service, responding promptly to complaints, or analyzing marketing campaigns.

Step 2: Data Collection

- **Utilize monitoring tools:** Apply AI and data analytics tools to gather data from social media platforms such as Facebook, Twitter, Instagram, and LinkedIn.
- **Integrate data:** Store and organize data from multiple sources for easy analysis and tracking.

Step 3: Data Analysis

- **Semantic analysis:** Use natural language processing (NLP) algorithms to understand feedback content, assess sentiment, and classify posts.
- **Trend detection:** Identify prominent trends in user feedback and behavior on social media to evaluate the popularity of various topics.

Step 4: Assess Impact

- **Monitor campaign effectiveness:** Use AI to measure the performance of marketing campaigns on social media, generating detailed reports on user engagement and content effectiveness.

- **Sentiment analysis:** Evaluate customer sentiment regarding the brand and products to adjust marketing and brand management strategies.

Step 5: Timely Response

- **Provide quick responses:** Utilize automated systems to respond immediately to customer inquiries, feedback, and complaints.
- **Improve customer service:** Identify common issues and quickly provide solutions to enhance customer satisfaction.

3. Practical Applications

- **Brand management:** Monitor brand reputation on social media to adjust strategies promptly to protect the brand image.
- **Predict market trends:** Analyze posts and interactions to anticipate future consumer needs and behaviors.

4. Benefits of Using AI in Social Media Monitoring

- **Rapid response:** AI enables businesses to react promptly to emerging trends and issues, maintaining customer engagement.
- **Enhanced customer insight:** In-depth analysis of customer opinions and sentiments helps businesses improve their products and services.
- **Time and resource savings:** Automating monitoring and analysis processes reduces the effort and time needed to track social media activities.

5. Conclusion

Social media monitoring using AI is a powerful tool for businesses in managing their brand and enhancing customer experiences. By timely tracking and responding to activities on social media, businesses can improve marketing effectiveness, protect their brand, and foster better relationships with customers. As AI technology continues to evolve, social media monitoring will become increasingly vital and essential in the business strategies of companies.

Idea No25. Marketing Planning Using AI

1. Introduction

Strategic marketing planning is an essential part of any business aiming to succeed in today's competitive marketplace. Utilizing artificial intelligence (AI) in this process not only helps businesses predict trends but also optimizes marketing campaigns based on historical data. AI can analyze information from previous campaigns, gain deeper insights into customer behavior, and assist in making more accurate decisions.

2. Steps to Implement Marketing Planning Using AI

Step 1: Data Collection

- **Compile historical data:** Gather data from previous marketing campaigns, including conversion rates, performance of communication channels, and customer information.
- **Diverse data sources:** Include data from social media, websites, email marketing, and market research.

Step 2: Data Analysis

- **Utilize AI for analysis:** Apply machine learning algorithms to analyze historical data to uncover behavioral patterns and market trends.
- **Identify success factors:** Analyze which factors contributed to the success or failure of past campaigns to learn from those experiences.

Step 3: Trend Prediction

- **Model future scenarios:** Based on historical data, AI can build predictive models that help forecast upcoming consumer trends and market demands.
- **Competitive analysis:** Monitor competitor activities and the market landscape to identify future opportunities and challenges.

Step 4: Campaign Planning

- **Build a multi-channel marketing plan:** Based on data analysis, plan for different communication channels (such as social media, online advertising, email marketing) strategically.
- **Determine the budget:** Use predictive analysis to allocate appropriate budgets for each channel, optimizing costs.

Step 5: Monitoring and Adjusting

- **Track campaign performance:** Utilize AI to monitor the performance of marketing campaigns after implementation, making timely adjustments as needed.
- **Learn from new data:** Continuously analyze the data collected from ongoing campaigns to improve future efforts.

3. Practical Applications

- **Email marketing:** AI tools can automatically analyze data from previous email campaigns and optimize the content for the next emails.
- **Targeted advertising:** Use AI to determine target audiences for ads based on behavioral and preference analysis of consumers.

4. Benefits of Using AI in Marketing Planning

- **Data-driven decisions:** AI enables making decisions based on data, reducing subjective decision-making.

- **Enhanced campaign effectiveness:** Accurate trend predictions help optimize campaigns, leading to increased conversion rates.
- **Time savings:** Automating the analysis and planning process saves time for the marketing team.

5. Conclusion

Utilizing AI in marketing planning offers numerous benefits for businesses, from optimizing campaigns to making data-driven decisions. With increasing competition in the modern market, AI helps businesses improve outcomes and gain a better understanding of their customers and market. Thus, AI has become an indispensable tool in the marketing strategies of contemporary businesses.

Idea No26. Organizing Events Using AI

1. Introduction

Event organization is an essential part of marketing strategies and brand building for many businesses. Utilizing artificial intelligence (AI) to analyze participant needs and plan appropriate events helps optimize guest experiences while enhancing the effectiveness of the event. AI can provide valuable insights into participants' preferences, behaviors, and trends, enabling organizers to make more informed decisions.

2. Steps to Implement AI in Event Organization

Step 1: Collect Participant Demand Data

- **Identify data sources:** Use survey tools, social media, and online behavior analysis to gather information about preferences and needs of guests.
- **Accumulate historical data:** If events have been organized in the past, collect data from these events for analysis.

Step 2: Data Analysis

- **Utilize AI for analysis:** Apply machine learning algorithms to analyze customer data, helping to identify behavioral patterns and trends.
- **Classify participant demographics:** Use AI to categorize participants based on age, interests, and event attendance needs.

Step 3: Event Planning

- **Define content and format:** Based on analysis, determine the content and format of the event (workshops, panel discussions, exhibitions, etc.) that aligns with participant needs.
- **Choose venue and timing:** Select the venue and timing for the event based on popularity and accessibility for the target audience.

Step 4: Optimize Attendee Experience

- **Personalize experiences:** Use analyzed information to tailor the experience for each attendee, such as suggesting notable sessions or relevant information.
- **Intelligent interaction:** Provide AI tools for attendees to interact with the event through mobile apps or online platforms.

Step 5: Evaluate Event Effectiveness

- **Collect feedback:** Use post-event surveys to gather opinions from participants, assessing the effectiveness of the event.
- **Analyze results:** Apply AI to analyze feedback data and extract lessons for future events.

3. Practical Applications

- **Online seminars:** Use AI to predict attendance numbers and select content suitable for different participant groups.
- **Trade shows:** Utilize AI analytics to optimize booth arrangements and event layout to attract more attendees.

4. Benefits of Using AI in Event Organization

- **Enhance customer experience:** Personalizing and optimizing the experience for participants increases satisfaction and customer retention.
- **Data-driven decisions:** Make organizational decisions based on real data, minimizing the risk of unsuccessful events.
- **Optimize the organizational process:** Automating some event organization processes saves time and costs for organizers.

5. Conclusion

Using AI in event organization helps businesses improve not just the preparation process but also in creating impressive experiences for participants. By analyzing participants' needs and behaviors, organizers can plan events that attract interest and increase effectiveness. In today's competitive landscape, AI has become a crucial tool in successfully organizing and managing events.

Idea No27. Channel Distribution Analysis Using AI

1. Introduction

In a competitive business environment, selecting and optimizing distribution channels is essential to ensure that products or services reach consumers effectively. Utilizing artificial intelligence (AI) in channel distribution analysis helps businesses evaluate the performance of each channel, allowing data-driven decisions to improve the distribution process.

2. Steps to Implement AI in Channel Distribution Analysis

Step 1: Data Collection

- **Identify distribution channels:** Create a list of current distribution channels the business is using, such as traditional retail, e-commerce, agents, etc.
- **Gather data:** Collect relevant data regarding the performance of these channels, including revenue, costs, sales volume, and customer interactions.

Step 2: Data Analysis

- **Utilize AI for analysis:** Apply machine learning algorithms and big data analytics to gain deeper insights into the performance of each channel. Models can also help uncover factors affecting channel efficiency.
- **Calculate key performance metrics:** Evaluate metrics such as delivery times, logistics costs, return rates, and customer experience across channels.

Step 3: Evaluate Channel Effectiveness

- **Compare performance:** Assess distribution channels based on the analyzed metrics to identify which channels are performing best and which need improvement.
- **Demand analysis:** Use AI to predict consumer trends and market demand to better align distribution channels.

Step 4: Suggest Improvements

- **Optimize processes:** Based on data analysis, provide recommendations to enhance operational processes within distribution channels, which may include adjusting pricing, improving customer service, or changing delivery methods.
- **Investment direction:** Identify potential channels that require more investment based on performance analysis and growth potential.

Step 5: Monitor and Adjust

- **Continuous evaluation:** Establish a continuous monitoring system to track the performance of

distribution channels over time, allowing the business to adjust strategies promptly.
- **Learn from new data:** Utilize AI to leverage data generated from ongoing distribution channels to improve processes.

3. Practical Applications

- **Multi-channel retailing:** Use AI to analyze the performance of physical stores versus online platforms to optimize sales strategies.
- **Inventory management:** AI can help optimize inventory management by analyzing demand across different distribution channels, minimizing stockouts or overstock situations.

4. Benefits of Using AI in Channel Distribution Analysis

- **Data-driven decisions:** Helps businesses make more accurate decisions regarding distribution channels based on detailed and actual information.
- **Cost optimization:** Analyzing the effectiveness of channels helps minimize operational costs and increase profitability.
- **Enhanced customer experience:** Improving consumer experience through optimized distribution channels allows for quicker and more effective responses to customer needs.

5. Conclusion

Utilizing AI in channel distribution analysis provides clear benefits to businesses, from optimizing costs to enhancing customer experience. By evaluating the effectiveness of different distribution channels, businesses can make strategic decisions that enhance competitiveness and create added value for customers. AI will continue to play a crucial role in the development and optimization of business distribution strategies in the future.

Idea No28. Evaluating ROI Using AI

1. Introduction

Evaluating the return on investment (ROI) of marketing campaigns is an essential factor in determining the feasibility and effectiveness of marketing activities. Utilizing artificial intelligence (AI) in this process enhances analytical capabilities, providing insights into the performance of each campaign, thereby making more optimized decisions regarding budget and marketing strategy.

2. Steps to Implement AI in ROI Evaluation

Step 1: Define Campaign Objectives

- **Analyze specific goals:** Before proceeding with the evaluation, clearly identify the goals of each marketing campaign, such as increasing sales, enhancing brand awareness, or generating leads.
- **Set KPIs:** Establish key performance indicators (KPIs) to monitor the success of the campaign.

Step 2: Data Collection

- **Cost data:** Record all costs associated with the campaign, such as advertising, personnel, technology, and other incidental expenses.
- **Revenue data:** Collect information regarding the revenue generated from the campaign, including sales volume, average order value, and revenue from new customers.

Step 3: Data Analysis

- **Utilize AI for analysis:** Apply machine learning algorithms to analyze the correlation between costs and revenues, providing a comprehensive overview of each campaign's ROI.

- **Multi-dimensional analysis:** AI can perform multi-dimensional analyses, examining factors such as timing, media channels, and target audiences affecting campaign performance.

Step 4: Make Evaluations

- **Calculate ROI:** Use the ROI formula: ROI = (Revenue - Cost) / Cost to determine whether the campaign is profitable. AI can automate this calculation process for large-scale campaigns.
- **Classify performance:** Use sentiment analysis and customer feedback from social media and surveys to generate detailed reports on campaign performance.

Step 5: Optimize Future Campaigns

- **Develop improvement strategies:** Based on ROI analysis, identify areas that need enhancement in upcoming marketing campaigns, such as optimizing budget allocation to more effective channels.
- **Learn from data:** Use insights and data from current campaigns to adjust and improve future campaigns.

3. Practical Applications

- **Online advertising:** Use AI to monitor and analyze the performance of online ad campaigns on platforms like Facebook, Google Ads, and others.
- **Email marketing:** Apply AI to analyze the effectiveness of email marketing campaigns in order to optimize content and timing based on feedback and open rates.

4. Benefits of Using AI in ROI Evaluation

- **Accurate analysis:** AI provides more accurate and detailed analysis results regarding campaign performance based on real data.

- **Enhanced decision-making capability:** Clear ROI analysis results help managers identify the most effective channels and campaigns.
- **Time savings:** Automating the analysis and reporting processes saves time for the marketing team and allows them to focus on improvement and creative strategies.

5. Conclusion

Utilizing AI in evaluating ROI for marketing campaigns offers numerous benefits to businesses, from cost optimization to enhancing campaign effectiveness. Through precise analysis and performance evaluation, businesses can make smarter decisions, improve competitiveness, and achieve their business objectives. AI will continue to play a crucial role in enhancing the effectiveness of marketing activities in the future.

Idea No29. Content Marketing Using AI

1. Introduction

Content marketing is a crucial strategy for attracting and retaining customers by providing valuable information. With the development of artificial intelligence (AI), creating engaging content has become faster and more efficient than ever. AI has the capability to analyze markets, identify trends, and generate diverse content such as blog posts, infographics, videos, and many other formats.

2. Steps to Implement AI in Content Marketing

Step 1: Market Research and Analysis

- **Identify target audience:** Use AI to analyze customer data, understanding their needs, preferences, and consumer behaviors.
- **Identify trends:** AI can monitor current trends and topics within the industry to help create timely and relevant content.

Step 2: Content Drafting

- **Utilize AI writing tools:** Tools such as GPT-3, Jasper, or Grammarly can assist in automatically generating blog posts, creating high-quality content quickly based on identified keywords and topics.
- **Design infographics:** AI can be used to automate graphic design, leveraging collected data to create unique and engaging infographics.

Step 3: Optimize Content

- **SEO and keywords:** AI has the capability to analyze effective keywords and optimize content for search engines. Tools like SEMrush or Ahrefs can assist in finding related keywords and evaluating competition.
- **Adjust tone and style:** AI can suggest changes to tone and writing style to better align with the target audience.

Step 4: Content Publishing and Promotion

- **Schedule publishing:** Utilize AI to optimize the timing and schedule for publishing content based on consumer feedback data, ensuring maximum reach.
- **Content distribution:** Use social media platforms and email to share content, leveraging AI to analyze the effectiveness of each distribution channel.

Step 5: Evaluate and Improve

- **Performance analysis:** AI can track and analyze content performance, assessing metrics such as traffic, time on page, click-through rates, and user interactions.
- **Learn from feedback:** Based on analysis, businesses can adjust their content strategies, enhancing the creation and sharing of content in the future.

3. Practical Applications

- **Blog writing:** Use AI to write and optimize blog posts, reducing content production time while maintaining quality.
- **Infographics:** Automatically create engaging infographics from large data sets, easily presenting information visually and effectively.

4. Benefits of Using AI in Content Marketing

- **Increased production efficiency:** Quickly generate high-quality content without requiring significant effort from creative teams.
- **Improved accuracy:** AI helps ensure that content meets the real needs of customers and aligns with market trends.
- **Optimized content strategy:** Analyzing data from previous campaigns aids in improving future content and optimizing ROI for marketing campaigns.

5. Conclusion

Utilizing AI in content marketing offers significant benefits for businesses, from saving time in content production to optimizing user experiences. With its ability to analyze and create effective content, AI will continue to play a pivotal role in enhancing the quality and effectiveness of content marketing campaigns in the future. Businesses that adopt AI can not only compete better but also build strong brands through quality content.

Idea No30. Analyzing Potential Customers Using AI

1. Introduction

Analyzing potential customers is an essential aspect of any business's marketing and sales strategy. Using artificial intelligence (AI) to identify and analyze potential customers allows businesses to optimize their sales processes, increase conversion rates, and develop relationships with customers. AI has the capability to process large amounts of data and detect patterns and trends that may not be easily recognized by humans.

2. Steps to Implement AI in Analyzing Potential Customers

Step 1: Data Collection

- **Data sources:** Gather data from various sources such as CRM (Customer Relationship Management) systems, social media, customer surveys, and transaction data.
- **Qualitative and quantitative data:** Collect both qualitative data (such as customer feedback) and quantitative data (such as transaction history and demographic information).

Step 2: Customer Classification

- **Utilize classification algorithms:** Apply machine learning algorithms to classify potential customers based on criteria such as shopping behavior, product needs, or brand interaction levels.
- **Identify common characteristics:** Analyze to identify common characteristics of potential customer groups, which helps shape targeting strategies.

Step 3: Predicting Customer Behavior

- **Predictive modeling:** Use AI models to predict potential customer buying behaviors and future needs by analyzing transaction history and online behaviors.
- **Engagement and relationships:** Evaluate customer engagement and interest levels toward the brand to identify high conversion potential.

Step 4: Optimize Targeting Strategies

- **Customer segmentation:** Based on analysis, create customer segments to design specific marketing campaigns for each group.
- **Personalized outreach campaigns:** Utilize analytical insights to develop personalized marketing campaigns targeting potential customers with relevant content.

Step 5: Evaluate and Improve

- **Monitor performance:** Use AI to track and evaluate the performance of potential customer outreach campaigns, determining what works well and what does not.
- **Learn from data:** Adjust and refine predictive models based on feedback and data from previous campaigns.

3. Practical Applications

- **Email marketing:** Use AI to analyze customer data and send marketing emails to those most likely interested in products or services.
- **CRM integration:** Integrate AI into CRM systems to automatically identify and classify potential customers based on online behavior and transaction data.

4. Benefits of Using AI in Analyzing Potential Customers

- **Enhanced accuracy:** AI can process and analyze large volumes of data to identify those potential customers with the highest likelihood of conversion, thereby minimizing risks in the sales process.
- **Time savings:** Automating the processes of identifying and analyzing potential customers allows sales teams to save time and focus on building relationships with customers.
- **Improved conversion rates:** With accurate and personalized information, the likelihood of converting potential customers increases.

5. Conclusion

Utilizing AI in analyzing potential customers offers significant benefits to businesses, from enhancing sales effectiveness to improving customer experiences. By predicting and analyzing buying behaviors, businesses can optimize targeting strategies and build stronger relationships with customers. AI not only helps businesses enhance their competitiveness but also creates better value for customers in their interactions with the brand.

Idea No31. Predicting Customer Reactions Using AI

1. Introduction

Predicting customer reactions to marketing campaigns is a crucial factor in optimizing communication effectiveness and sales strategies. Artificial intelligence (AI) can analyze historical data and consumer behavior, thereby making accurate predictions about how customers might react to specific marketing initiatives. This not only helps businesses improve their strategies but also delivers greater value to customers.

2. Steps to Implement AI in Predicting Customer Reactions

Step 1: Data Collection

- **Historical data:** Gather data from previous marketing campaigns, including customer information, campaign content, media channels, and results.
- **Behavioral data:** Collect behavioral data of customers from digital platforms, including website interactions, social media feedback, and transaction behavior.

Step 2: Data Analysis

- **Utilize analytical algorithms:** Apply machine learning algorithms to analyze data and uncover response patterns of customers toward different types of campaigns.
- **Identify key factors:** Determine the critical factors influencing customer reactions, such as content, timing, and approach.

Step 3: Predicting Reactions

- **Predictive modeling:** Use AI to develop predictive models that estimate how likely customers are to engage,

respond, or make a purchase after encountering a specific campaign.
- **Customer segmentation:** Group customers into segments based on their likelihood of response, allowing for personalized campaigns for each group.

Step 4: Optimize Campaigns

- **Adjust content and approach:** Based on predictions, modify content elements and execution methods of campaigns to enhance their popularity and effectiveness.
- **Timing and outreach channels:** Use predictions to identify the optimal timing and distribution channels where customers are most likely to engage.

Step 5: Performance Evaluation and Improvement

- **Monitor actual responses:** Compare predictions with actual customer reactions to evaluate the accuracy of the models.
- **Improve models:** Based on feedback and actual results, refine and update predictive models to enhance accuracy for future campaigns.

3. Practical Applications

- **Online advertising:** Use AI to predict consumer reactions to advertisements on social media or search platforms, then adjust targeting and ad content accordingly.
- **Email marketing campaigns:** Based on predictions, personalize email content and sending times to optimize open and click-through rates.

4. Benefits of Using AI in Predicting Customer Reactions

- **Enhanced accuracy:** AI can process large volumes of data to provide precise and reliable predictions of customer reactions.

- **Time savings:** Automating the prediction process reduces the time and effort required for market research.
- **Increased ROI:** Accurate predictions help businesses optimize marketing campaigns, thereby enhancing return on investment (ROI).

5. Conclusion

Predicting customer reactions using AI is an effective method for businesses to optimize their marketing campaigns. By analyzing customer behavior and historical data, predictive models can create better strategies tailored to customer needs and preferences. The application of AI not only enhances predictive accuracy but also delivers greater value to customers while strengthening the competitive edge of businesses in the modern market.

Idea No32. Running Real-Time Advertising Using AI

1. Introduction

Real-time bidding (RTB) is an online advertising method that allows the buying and selling of advertisements to occur instantaneously through advertising exchanges. Utilizing artificial intelligence (AI) in this process helps optimize ads based on performance, thereby improving the effectiveness of advertising campaigns and increasing ROI (return on investment).

2. Steps to Implement AI in Running Real-Time Advertising

Step 1: Data Collection and Analysis

- **Data from multiple sources:** Gather data from various advertising platforms, websites, social media, and previous advertising campaigns to gain an overall view of performance.
- **Analysis of user behavior:** Use AI to analyze user behavior across different platforms to understand how they interact with advertisements.

Step 2: Setting Campaign Goals

- **Define KPIs:** Establish key performance indicators (KPIs) such as click-through rate (CTR), cost per click (CPC), and conversion rate.
- **Target audience:** Utilize analytical data to identify the target audience for ads based on demographics, interests, and behaviors.

Step 3: Automated Ad Optimization

- **Optimization algorithms:** Apply machine learning algorithms to automatically adjust budgets, refine target audiences, and change ad content in real-time.
- **Performance analysis:** Monitor ad performance across various time frames to quickly identify changes in customer behavior and adjust campaigns accordingly.

Step 4: Predicting Outcomes

- **Predictive modeling:** Use AI to develop predictive models that estimate future ad campaign performance based on historical data and user behavior.
- **Risk analysis:** Assess risks related to ad decisions and optimize expenditures to minimize budget waste.

Step 5: Evaluation and Improvement

- **Monitoring and analysis:** Continuously track ad performance and use AI to analyze collected data, facilitating timely adjustments.
- **Process improvement:** Leverage feedback from previous campaigns to enhance and optimize ads for future campaigns.

3. Practical Applications

- **PPC Advertising (Pay-Per-Click):** Use AI on advertising platforms like Google Ads to optimize advertising budgets in real time based on performance.

- **Social Media Advertising:** Optimize ads on Facebook, Instagram, and other platforms by utilizing AI to adjust content and target audiences in real time.

4. Benefits of Using AI in Running Real-Time Advertising

- **Increased accuracy:** AI enhances the ability to predict and optimize ads, ensuring that the most effective advertisements are maximized.
- **Cost savings:** Automating the ad management process minimizes budget waste and increases spending efficiency.
- **Faster responses:** AI allows marketers to quickly respond and adjust campaigns based on changes in consumer behavior.

5. Conclusion

Running real-time advertising using AI is a powerful solution for businesses looking to optimize advertising and improve campaign effectiveness. By continuously collecting and analyzing data, AI enables businesses to make smarter and timely decisions, thereby increasing ROI and enhancing user experience. The integration of technology and marketing will continue to evolve, creating new opportunities for businesses in the digital age.

Idea No33. Multichannel Interaction Using AI

1. Introduction

Multichannel interaction is an increasingly important marketing strategy that allows businesses to engage with customers through various platforms and channels such as websites, social media, email, and mobile applications. Utilizing artificial intelligence (AI) in this process helps optimize customer experiences, create stronger connections, and enhance communication effectiveness.

2. Steps to Implement AI in Multichannel Interaction

Step 1: Customer Data Analysis

- **Data collection from multiple sources:** Gather data from interaction channels such as websites, emails, social media, and customer service calls to build a comprehensive customer profile.
- **Identifying behavior and preferences:** Use AI to analyze customer behavior and preferences to understand how they interact with different channels.

Step 2: Creating a Multichannel Customer Profile

- **Building a 360-degree customer profile:** Integrate information from multiple channels into a single profile, providing businesses with a holistic view of the customer.
- **Intelligent customer segmentation:** Use AI to segment customers based on behavior, preferences, and interaction history, creating suitable target groups.

Step 3: Automated and Personalized Interaction

- **Chatbots and virtual assistants:** Deploy AI-powered chatbots and virtual assistants to assist customers on websites and social media, providing instant information and answering queries.
- **Personalized content:** Use AI to create personalized content and marketing messages for each channel, ensuring customers receive a consistent and seamless experience.

Step 4: Monitoring and Optimizing Interaction

- **Performance analysis:** Utilize AI to monitor the performance of various interaction channels, analyzing data on engagement levels, customer feedback, and conversion rates.
- **Campaign optimization:** Based on analytical results, adjust and optimize marketing campaigns to improve interaction effectiveness.

Step 5: Evaluation and Improvement

- **Collecting feedback:** Continuously gather customer feedback across channels to better understand their experiences and identify areas for improvement.
- **Learning from data:** Use AI to learn from collected data to continuously enhance the interaction process and marketing content.

3. Practical Applications

- **Social media management:** Use AI to automate posting on social media platforms, track customer interactions, and quickly respond to questions or comments.
- **Email marketing:** Personalize content in email marketing based on customer behaviors and preferences, ensuring the content is relevant to each segment.

4. Benefits of Using AI in Multichannel Interaction

- **Improved customer experience:** Multichannel interaction allows customers to receive a continuous and coherent experience across all platforms.
- **Enhanced marketing effectiveness:** AI enables businesses to optimize marketing campaigns, improving conversion rates and ROI.
- **Time and resource savings:** Utilizing AI to automate interaction processes helps lighten the burden on staff and save resources.

5. Conclusion

Multichannel interaction using AI is a powerful solution for businesses to optimize communication with customers. By collecting and analyzing data from multiple sources, AI enables businesses to create personalized and seamless experiences for customers. The combination of technology and customer interaction will continue to evolve, creating new opportunities for businesses in the digital age.

Idea No34. Fraud Detection Using AI

1. Introduction

Fraudulent activities in marketing can cause significant harm to businesses, not only financially but also in terms of reputation. With technological advancements, fraudulent schemes are becoming increasingly sophisticated. Utilizing artificial intelligence (AI) to detect and prevent fraudulent behaviors helps protect marketing budgets and enhances the reliability of information and results obtained.

2. Steps to Implement AI in Fraud Detection

Step 1: Data Collection

- **Multidimensional data:** Gather data from various sources, including information from advertising campaigns, user behavior analysis, and customer feedback.
- **Transaction history:** Record transaction history and related customer information as a basis for analysis.

Step 2: Build Fraud Models

- **Utilizing machine learning algorithms:** Apply machine learning algorithms to build a fraud detection model that identifies suspicious behaviors based on historical behavior patterns.
- **Identify risk factors:** Analyze risk factors that may lead to fraud, such as click timing, interaction frequency, and abnormal activities compared to previous behaviors.

Step 3: Anomaly Detection

- **Anomaly analysis:** Use AI to monitor user behaviors in real time, detecting unusual activities that may indicate fraud.
- **Optimize processes:** Regularly update and adjust fraud detection models based on new data and feedback to ensure continuous improvement in detection capabilities.

Step 4: Alerting and Response

- **Automated alert systems:** Set up alert systems to notify management when the model detects suspicious behaviors, allowing for timely responses.
- **Response procedures:** Provide specific guidelines to address identified fraud situations, including suspending or adjusting advertising campaigns.

Step 5: Evaluate Effectiveness

- **Monitor results:** Assess the effectiveness of the fraud detection process by reviewing advertising campaigns and analyzing data before and after applying AI.
- **Analysis and improvement:** Use collected data to continuously enhance the models and fraud detection processes.

3. Practical Applications

- **E-commerce industry:** Use AI to detect fraudulent transactions in e-commerce, such as fake payments or fraudulent accounts.
- **Online advertising:** Monitor and detect click fraud or invalid traffic in online advertising campaigns.

4. Benefits of Using AI in Fraud Detection

- **Increased accuracy:** AI has the capability to detect complex fraud patterns that may be difficult for humans to identify.
- **Cost savings:** Preventing fraud before it occurs can lead to significant cost savings and increased ROI.
- **Brand protection:** Preventing fraudulent activities helps safeguard the company's reputation and build trust with customers.

5. Conclusion

Fraud detection using AI is an effective solution for protecting businesses from fraudulent activities in marketing. By applying advanced technologies to monitor and analyze user behaviors, businesses can quickly identify and prevent unusual activities. Investing in AI technology not only improves marketing effectiveness but also strengthens sustainable and informed business decisions.

Idea No35. Performance Analysis Using AI

1. Introduction

Performance analysis is a crucial step in evaluating the effectiveness of marketing campaigns. Monitoring and analyzing performance metrics provide businesses with clearer insights into their activities, allowing for timely adjustments to optimize results. Utilizing artificial intelligence (AI) in this process not only accelerates analysis but also enhances accuracy and efficiency.

2. Steps to Implement AI in Performance Analysis

Step 1: Data Collection

- **Diverse data sources:** Collect data from various sources such as social media, email, websites, online ads, and order data to obtain a comprehensive picture of your marketing activities.
- **Data formatting:** Ensure that data is properly formatted to facilitate a smooth analysis process.

Step 2: Identify Key Performance Indicators (KPIs)

- **Establish KPIs:** Identify the most important metrics to measure performance, such as conversion rates, cost per conversion, engagement rates, and revenue.
- **Set Specific Goals:** Clearly define objectives for each campaign to easily track progress.

Step 3: Analyze Data with AI

- **Utilize AI Algorithms:** Implement machine learning algorithms to analyze data and identify patterns, trends, and factors influencing campaign performance.
- **Segmentation and Analysis:** Use AI to segment customer groups and analyze how each group interacts with the campaign to gain deeper insights.

Step 4: Optimize Campaigns

- **Testing and Adjusting:** Use information gathered from analysis to make adjustments to campaigns, covering everything from content to advertising methods.
- **Immediate Feedback:** Implement timely adjustments throughout the campaign run to improve performance on the fly.

Step 5: Evaluate and Improve

- **Monitor Results:** After adjustments, continue to track performance metrics to assess the impact of the changes made.
- **Learn from Data:** Use collected information to refine the analysis process for future campaigns.

3. Practical Applications

- **Social Media Advertising:** Monitor engagement across platforms like Facebook or Instagram to adjust content and advertising budgets.
- **Email Marketing:** Analyze open and click-through rates to optimize content and timing for future email campaigns.

4. Benefits of Using AI in Performance Analysis

- **Increased Accuracy:** AI possesses the capability to analyze large datasets and provide more precise assessments than humans.

- **Time Savings:** Automated analysis saves time for marketing teams, allowing them to focus on more strategic activities.
- **Opportunity Detection:** AI can quickly identify new trends and market opportunities, enabling businesses to seize them promptly.

5. Conclusion

Performance analysis using AI is a powerful tool that aids businesses in monitoring and optimizing their marketing campaigns. By effectively and accurately analyzing data, companies can make smarter decisions, thereby increasing ROI and creating better customer experiences. Investing in AI technology not only brings immediate benefits but also shapes the future of marketing campaigns.

www.ingramcontent.com/pod-product-compliance
Lightning Source LLC
Chambersburg PA
CBHW030444220526
45464CB00006B/2413